This library edition published in 2012 by Walter Foster Publishing, Inc.
Walter Foster Library
Distributed by Black Rabbit Books.
P.O. Box 3263 Mankato, Minnesota 56002

Printed in Mankato, Minnesota, USA by CG Book Printers, a division of Corporate Graphics.

First Library Edition

Library of Congress Cataloging-in-Publication Data

Learn to draw insects.
    p. cm.
  "Illustrated by Diana Fisher."
  ISBN 978-1-936309-52-8
1. Insects in art--Juvenile literature. 2.
Drawing--Technique--Juvenile literature. I. Fisher, Diana, illustrator.
II. Walter Foster (Firm)
  NC783.L43 2012
  743.6'57--dc23

                                                                2011046085

052012
17679

9 8 7 6 5 4 3 2 1

learn to draw

Insects

Learn to draw and color 26 insects, step by easy step, shape by simple shape!

Illustrated by Diana Fisher

Getting Started

When you look closely at the drawings in this book, you'll notice that they're made up of basic shapes, such as circles, triangles, and rectangles. To draw all your favorite creatures, just start with simple shapes as you see here. It's easy and fun!

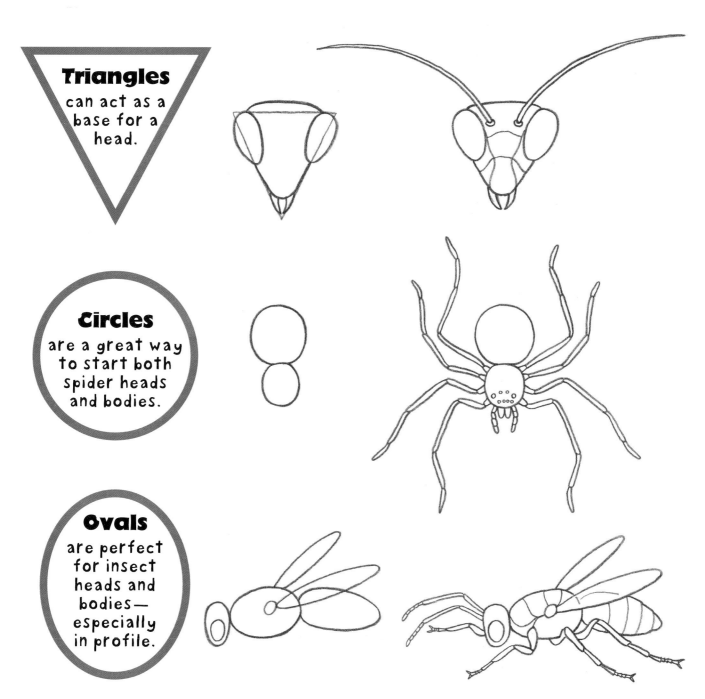

Triangles can act as a base for a head.

Circles are a great way to start both spider heads and bodies.

Ovals are perfect for insect heads and bodies— especially in profile.

Coloring Tips

There's more than one way to bring creepy crawlies to life on paper—you can use crayons, markers, or colored pencils. Be sure you have plenty of good "bug" colors—from black, brown, and green to bright red, blue, yellow, and orange!

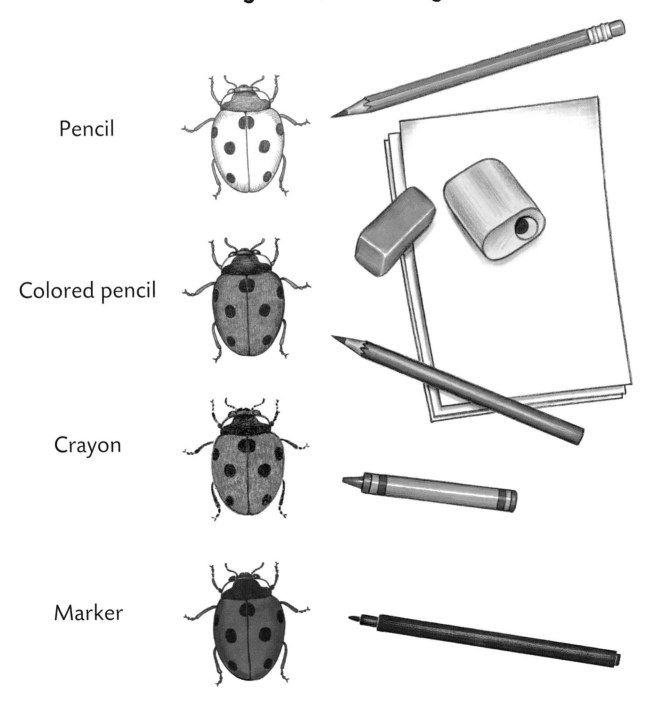

Pencil

Colored pencil

Crayon

Marker

3

Pill Millipede

Rolling up into a tight ball is what this bug does best! It hides its 15 pairs of legs and tucks in its head for protection.

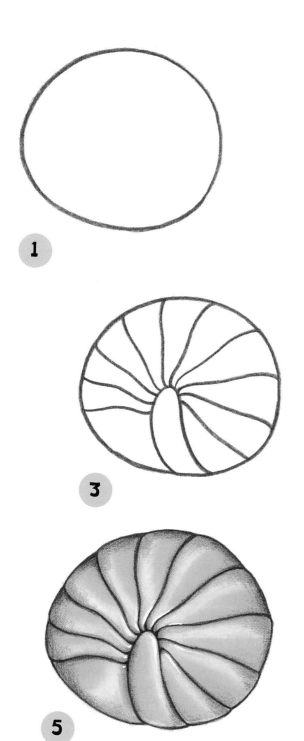

1

2

3

4

5

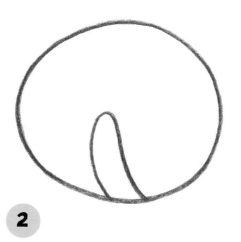

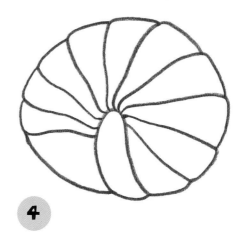

fun fact

Millipede means 1,000 feet, but no millipede has more than 750 legs. Although large species of pill millipedes can grow to the size of a tennis ball, millipedes in this order have only 30 legs.

Mexican Red-Legged Tarantula

Its red body and leg hairs make this furry critter stand out! Like all tarantulas, it has eight eyes, eight legs, and two pedipalps.

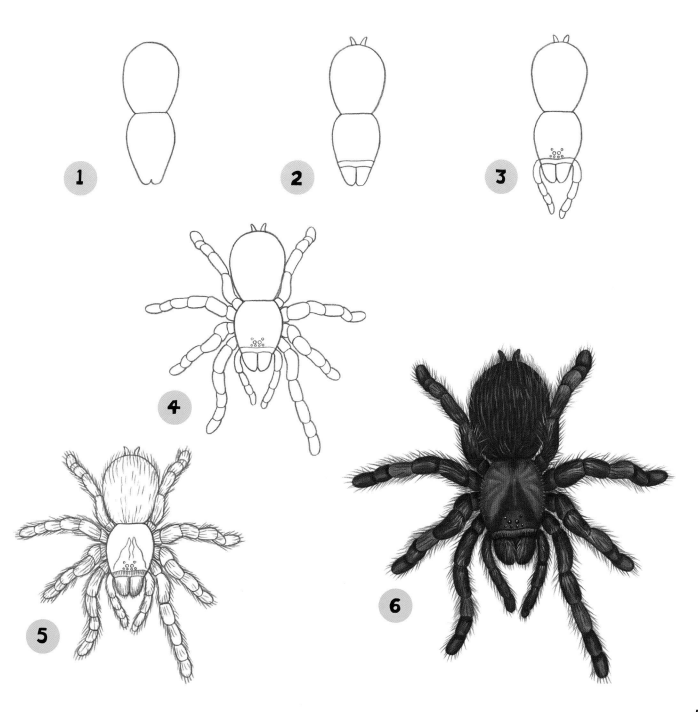

True Cricket

with a flat body and folded wings,
the cricket appears quite dull. But its beautiful
song makes it a favorite international pet.

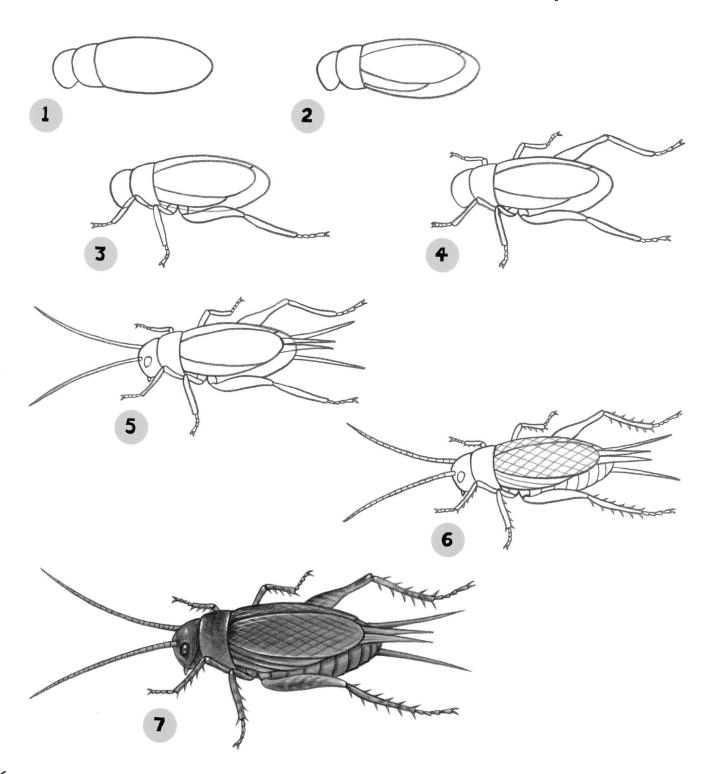

Walking Stick

This slender insect disguises itself among plants and trees. Brown coloring and a spiny, ridged body provide camouflage.

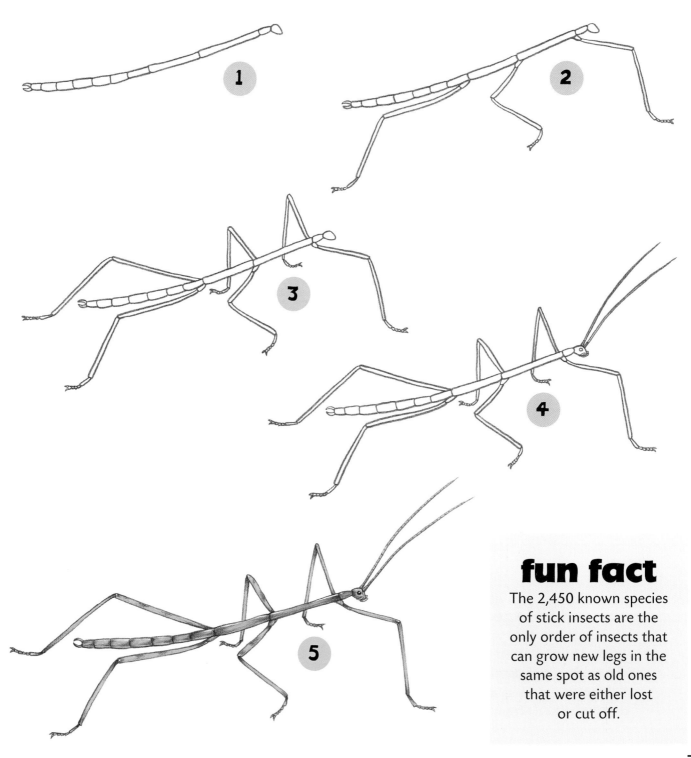

fun fact

The 2,450 known species of stick insects are the only order of insects that can grow new legs in the same spot as old ones that were either lost or cut off.

Stink Bug

Bold colors warn would-be predators that this shield bug tastes foul—if the bug's signature smell doesn't scare them off first!

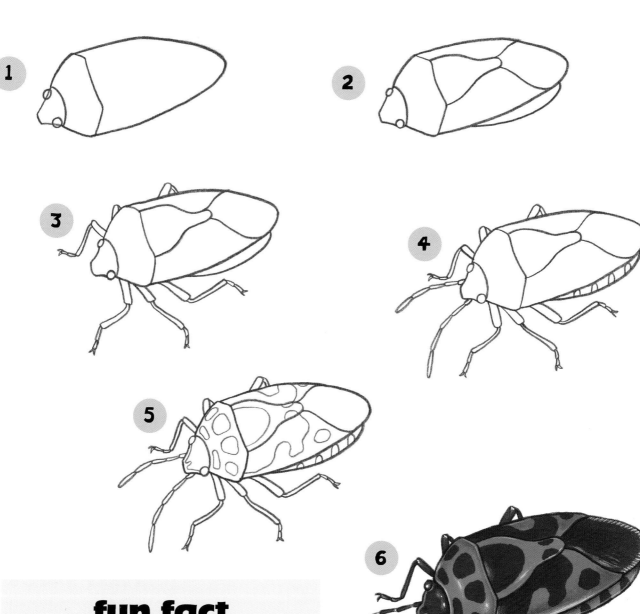

1

2

3

4

5

6

fun fact

Many bugs travel to warmer places in the winter because their bodies can't take the cold—but glycerol in the stink bug's bloodstream acts as an antifreeze, keeping its body from freezing in winter.

Treehopper

Also known as a thorn bug, the treehopper has a unique shape that provides a disguise and makes the bug difficult to eat!

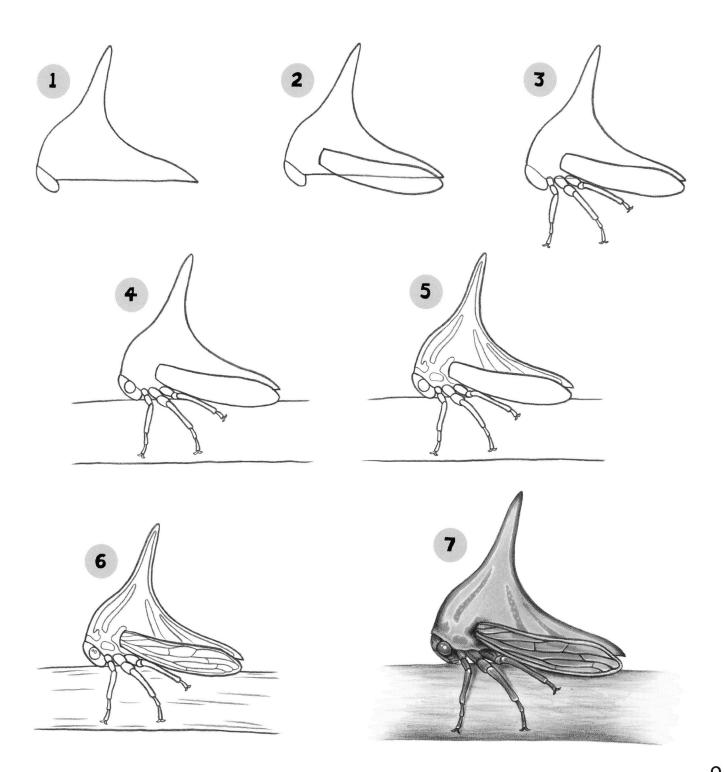

Luna Moth

All "moon" moths possess large, furry bodies with broad, long-tailed wings. But only the male sports feathered antennae!

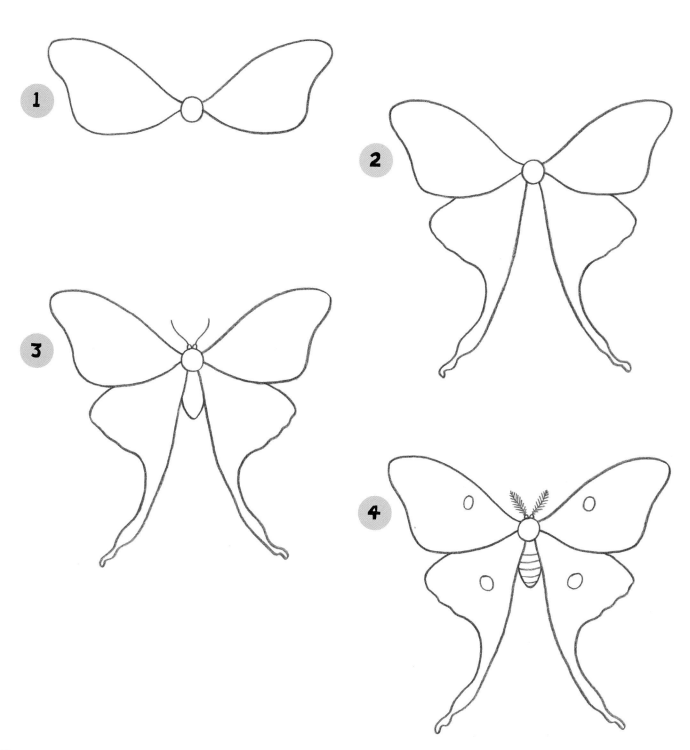

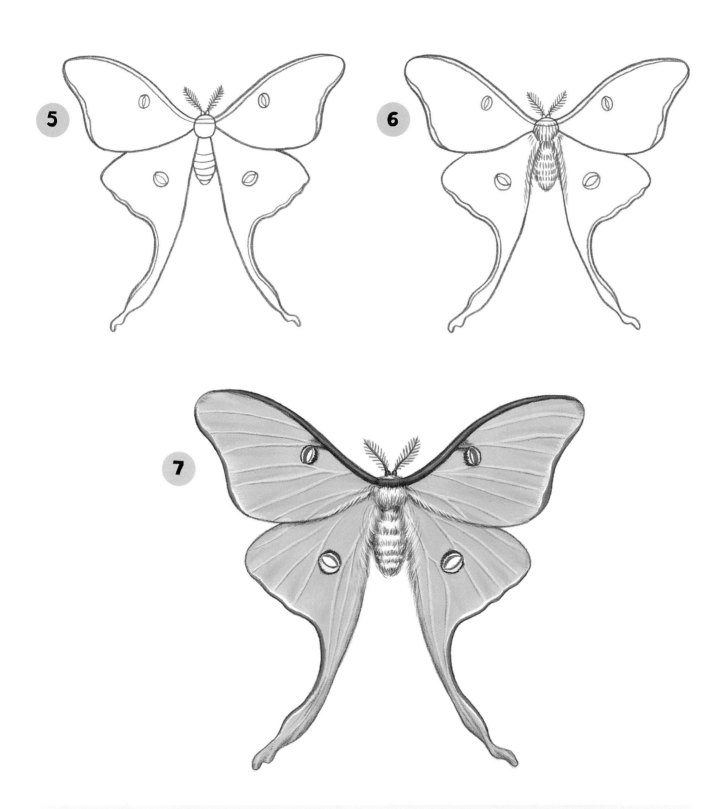

5

6

7

fun fact

This American saturnid moth species is named after the eyespots on its wings, which look like moons. It is alternately referred to as "luna," "lunar," and "moon" moth— all three names meaning exactly the same thing.

Spitting Spider

A domed body and symmetrical spots distinguish this arachnid—but its two large, spitting chelicerae are hard to ignore!

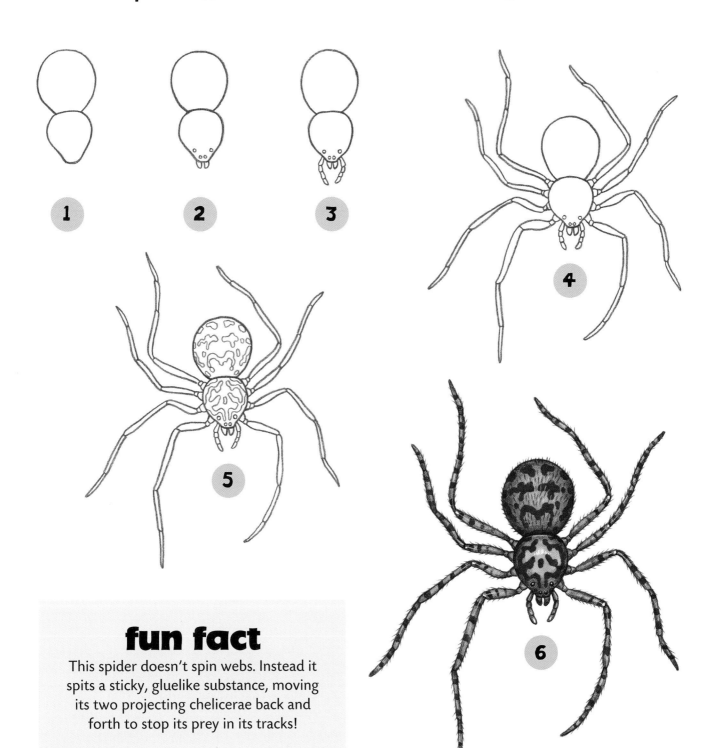

1

2

3

4

5

6

fun fact

This spider doesn't spin webs. Instead it spits a sticky, gluelike substance, moving its two projecting chelicerae back and forth to stop its prey in its tracks!

Broad-Winged Damselfly

Features like its round eyes and slender body are dragonfly-like, but the damsel's folded wing pairs are all its own!

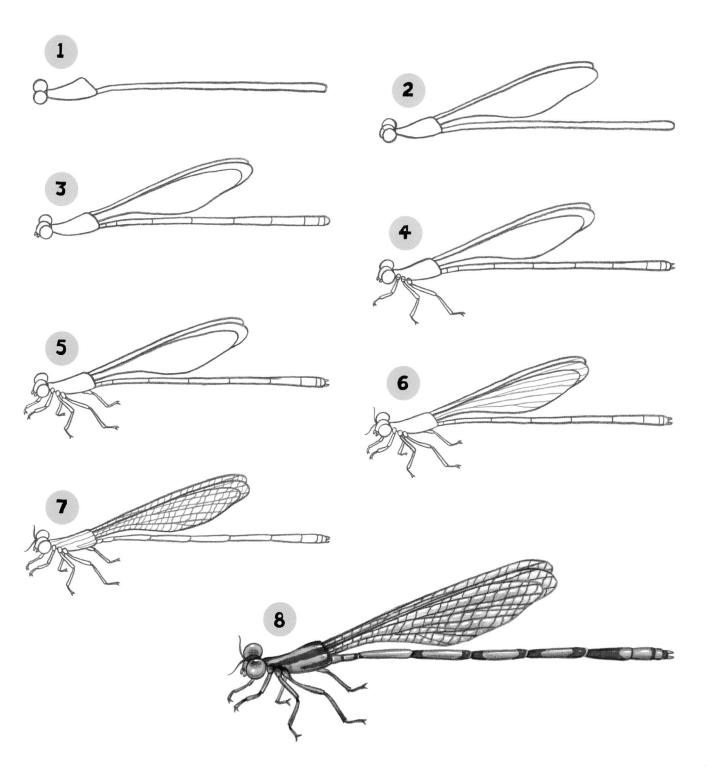

Chactid Scorpion

Pinching claws and a stinging tail separate
this arachnid from its spider cousins,
despite its pedipalps and eight legs.

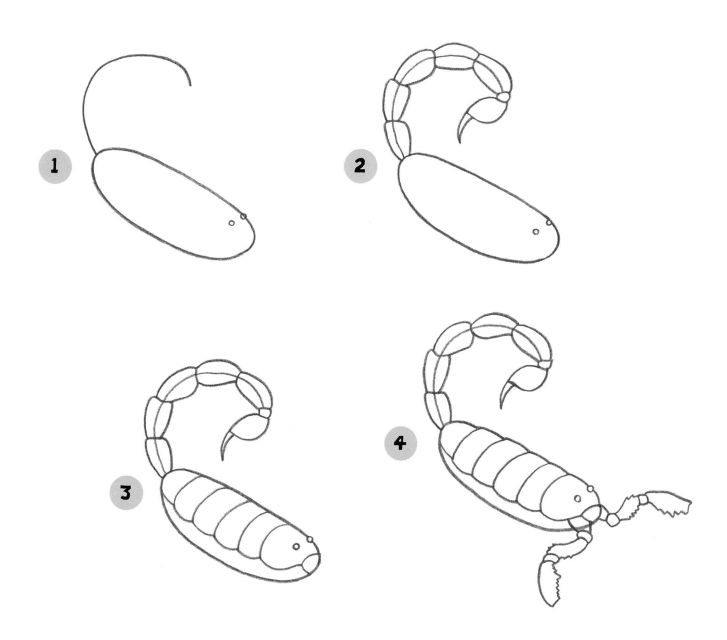

fun fact

Scorpions are famous for venomous stings—but out of 1,400
species of scorpions, only about two dozen are
truly dangerous to humans. The chactidae family have a beelike
sting, harmless unless an allergic reaction occurs.

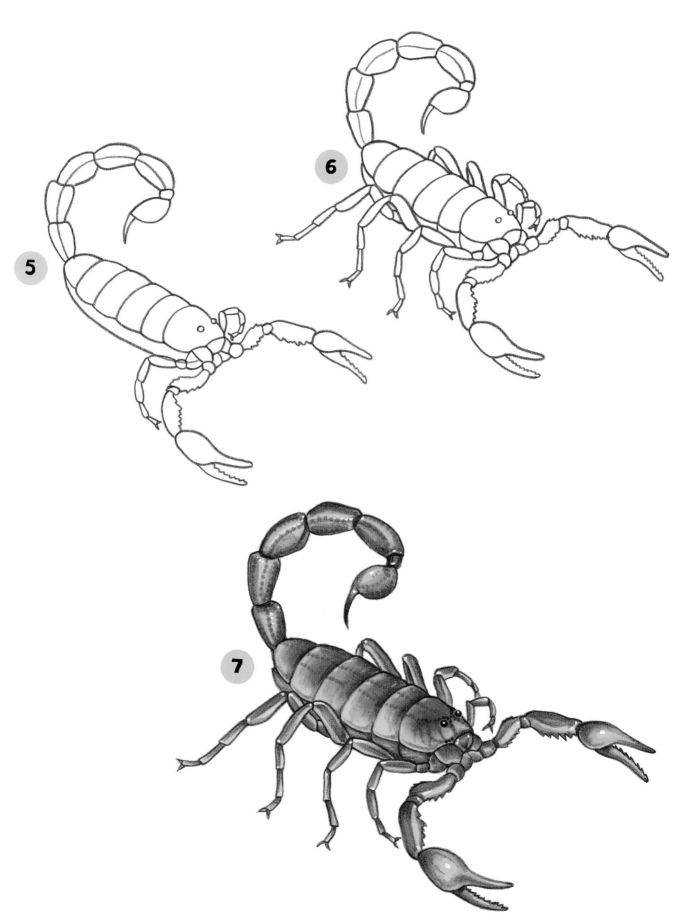

5

6

7

Fire Ant

The fire ant's bumpy tapered "waist" connects its upper body—or thorax—to its abdomen, where its stinger is located.

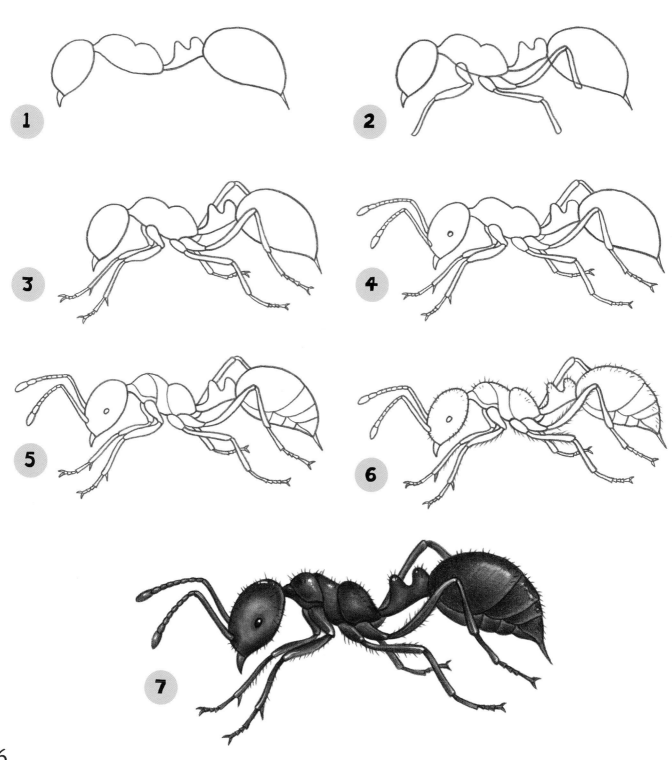

Higher Termite

The pale, snouted harvester termite has a dark, round head with a long, nozzle-like end. Worker termites have antennae but no eyes!

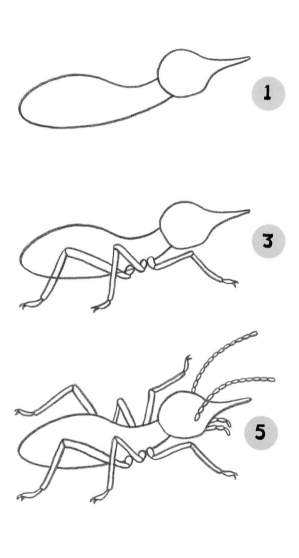

1

2

3

4

5

6

fun fact

Like the snouted harvester worker, the soldier termite has no eyes. But it's armed with large, biting jaws, and it can squirt a sticky poison from its snoutlike head!

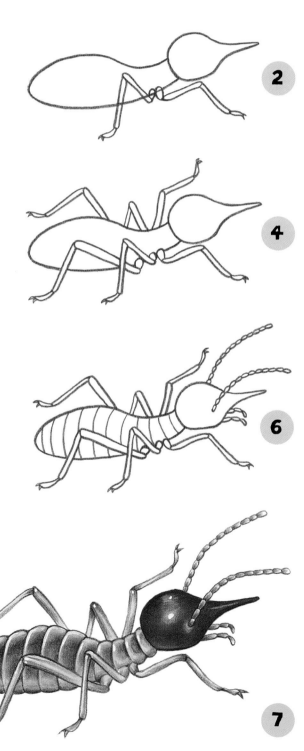

7

Scutigerid Centipede

This predator has large, compound eyes and poison claws. It's born with 14 legs and gains a new pair after each molt.

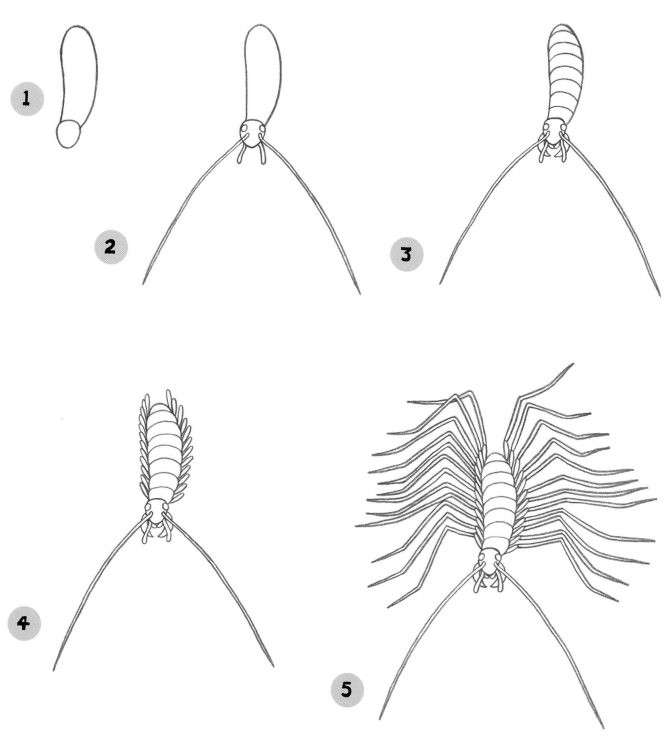

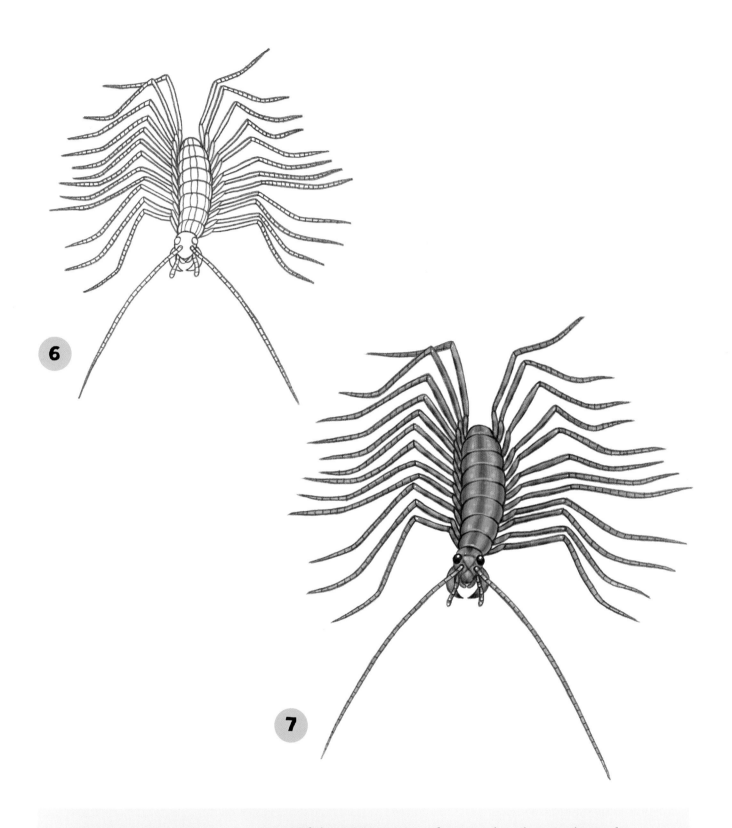

6

7

fun fact

Of the 3,000 species of centipedes, the members of the scutigeridae family are the quickest. In fact, these predators are some of the fastest insects around. They can run up to 16" per second—that's almost 1 mile per hour!

Life Stages

All animals change as they grow.
But some insects experience major changes
in appearance as they develop over time!

The honeybee starts out as an egg, laid by the queen. Once hatched, the egg becomes a pale, grublike larva. In the final larval stage, the bee is still pale, but closer to its final shape, which it reaches after 21 days.

The lightning bug, or firefly, develops from an egg into a wingless larva called a "glow worm." After eating for about three months, the larva digs a tunnel. Later it emerges from the ground as a fully developed beetle.

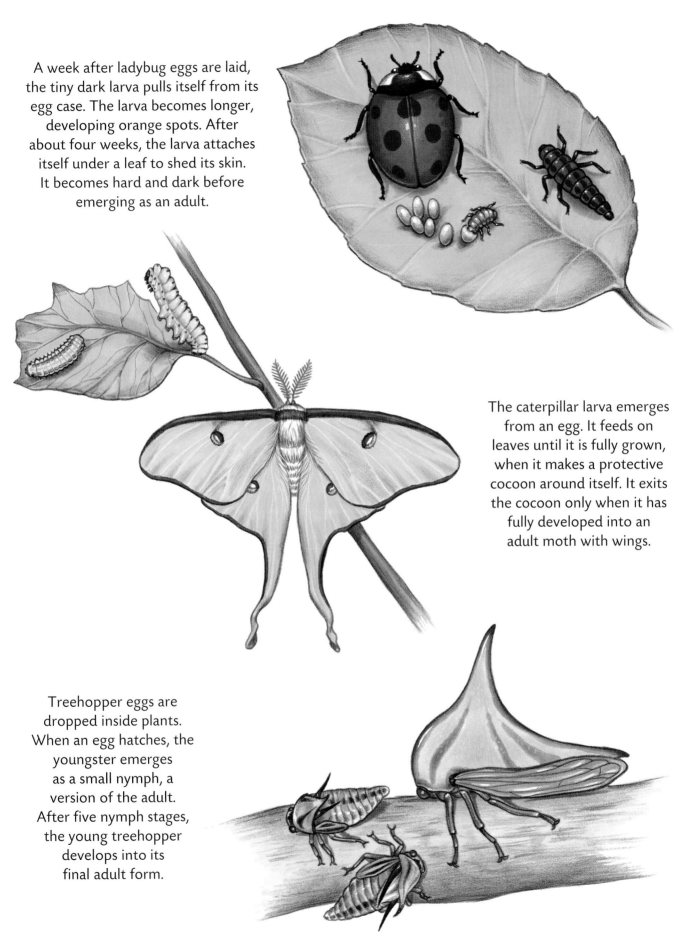

A week after ladybug eggs are laid, the tiny dark larva pulls itself from its egg case. The larva becomes longer, developing orange spots. After about four weeks, the larva attaches itself under a leaf to shed its skin. It becomes hard and dark before emerging as an adult.

The caterpillar larva emerges from an egg. It feeds on leaves until it is fully grown, when it makes a protective cocoon around itself. It exits the cocoon only when it has fully developed into an adult moth with wings.

Treehopper eggs are dropped inside plants. When an egg hatches, the youngster emerges as a small nymph, a version of the adult. After five nymph stages, the young treehopper develops into its final adult form.

Jewel Wasp

Known for its dimpled, hard body with metallic
coloring, this bright jewel of the bug world
is also known as a "ruby-tailed wasp."

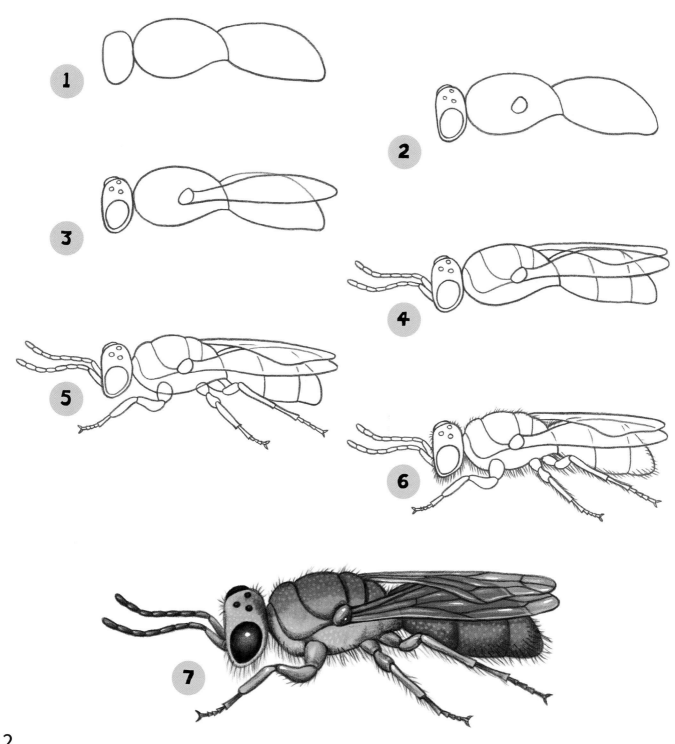

Fulgorid Bug

For a master of camouflage, this odd bug with a unique head shape sure stands out! It startles predators with its bright wings.

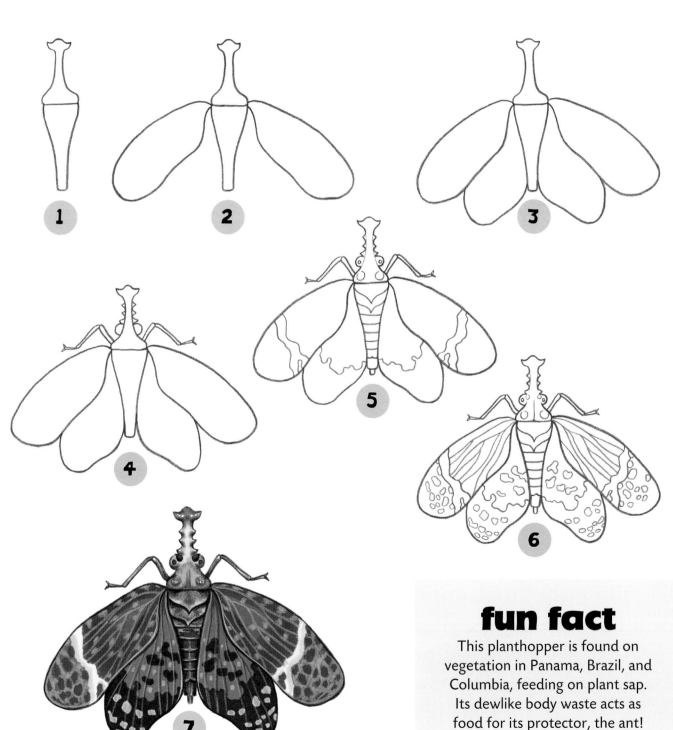

1

2

3

4

5

6

7

fun fact

This planthopper is found on vegetation in Panama, Brazil, and Columbia, feeding on plant sap. Its dewlike body waste acts as food for its protector, the ant!

23

Leaf Beetle

A shiny shell and flexible black legs
make the sagra species look almost robotic!
Its nickname is the jeweled frog beetle.

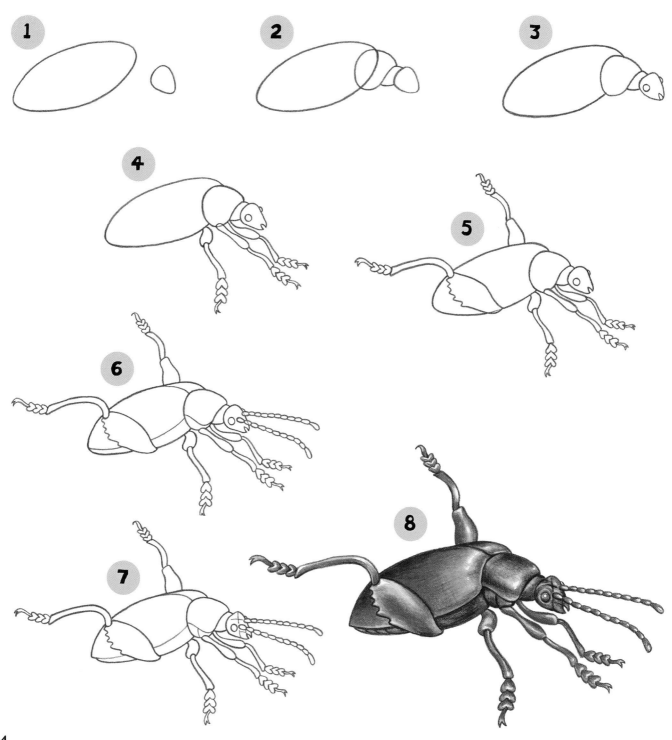

Acanthosomatid Bug

A Y-shaped mark on its thorax distinguishes this bug from other species with small heads and shield shapes!

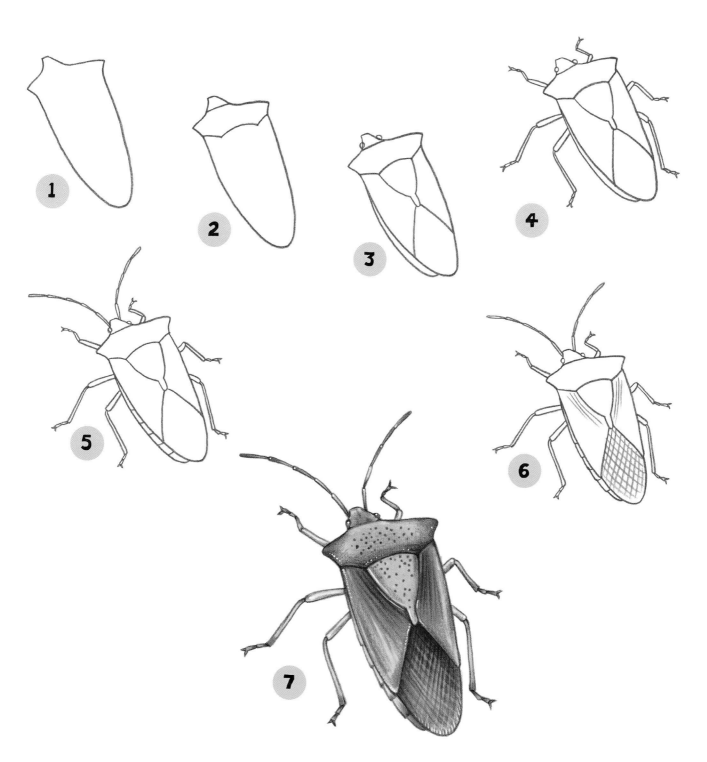

Praying Mantis

Natural coloring and leafy wings camouflage
the mantis, while large eyes, sharp leg spines,
and powerful jaws capture its prey.

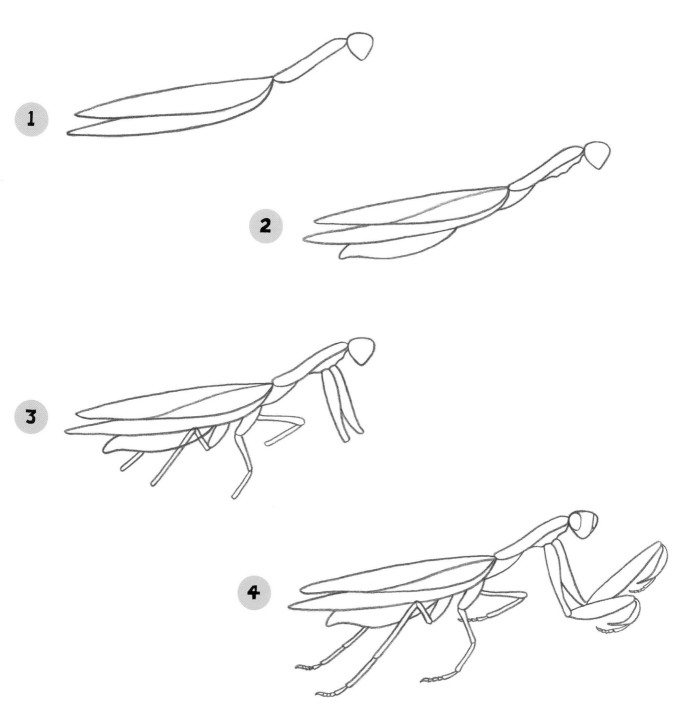

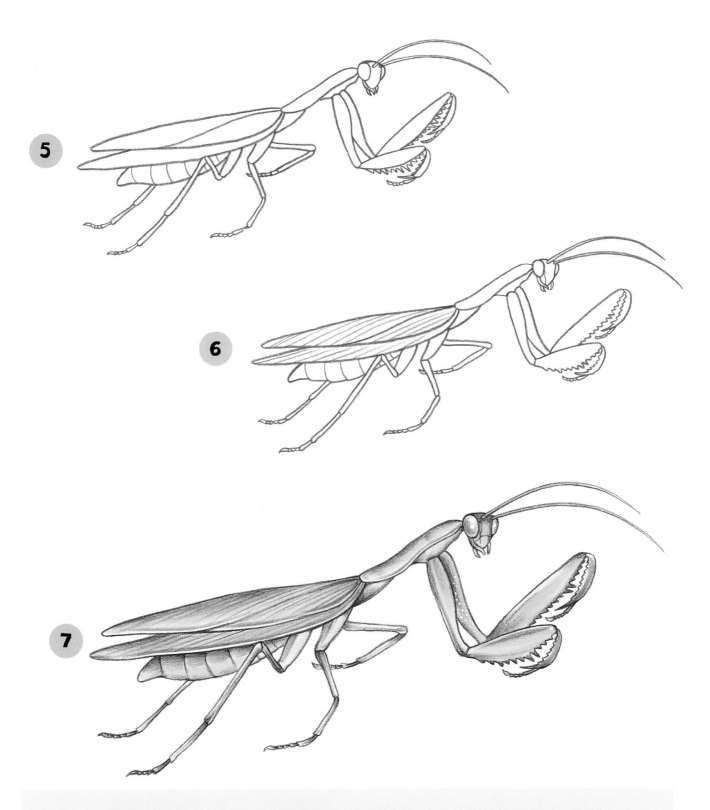

5

6

7

fun fact

Legend has it that the female praying mantis always eats the male mantis after mating. It's true that females will sometimes eat mates—especially if in captivity—but most males are not eaten by their partners.

Common Scorpionfly

Narrow, banded wings, a beaked head,
and a slender body distinguish this bug.
The male's abdomen has a scorpionlike tip.

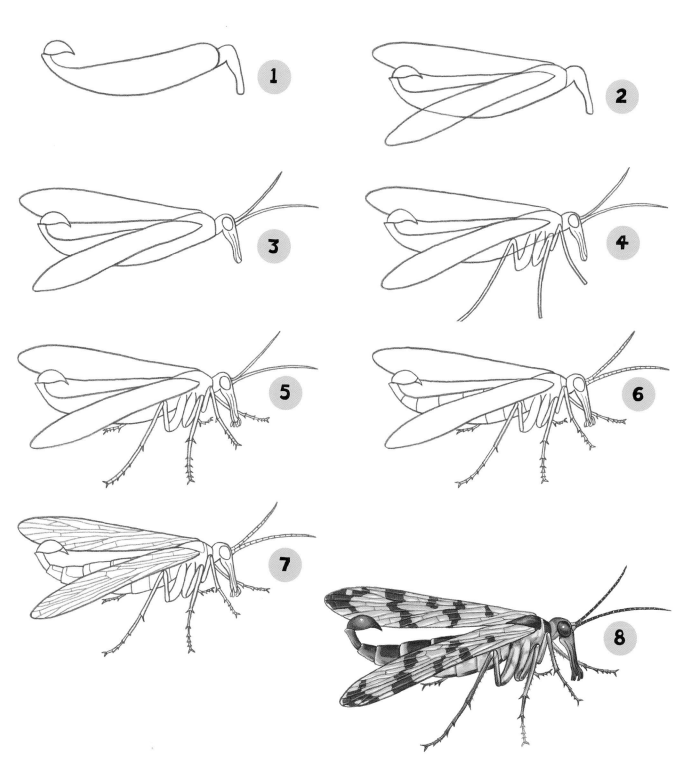

Katydid

with short wings, long legs, and bright green coloring, this bush cricket bears a strong resemblance to a grasshopper!

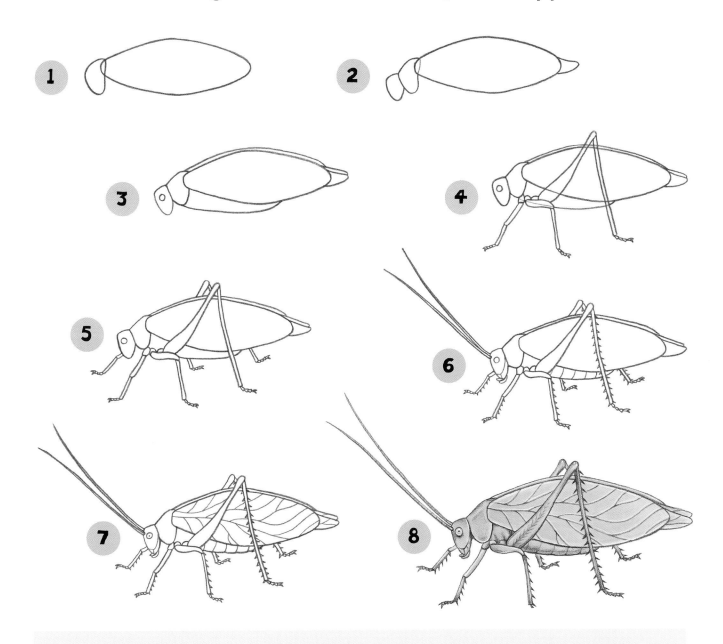

fun fact

The katydid is named for the sound it makes, a call that sounds like "katy did." Male katydids "sing" with the base of their front wings to attract mates, and females respond with a soft song of their own. These songs are heard through "eardrums" located in the katydid's front legs!

Violin Beetle

Long and flat, this member of the
ground beetle set gets its common name
from its head and body outline.

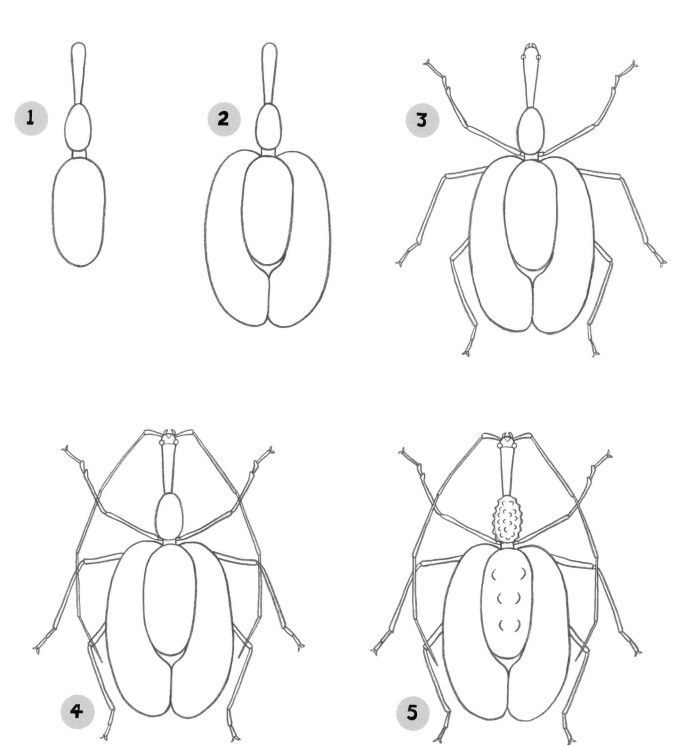

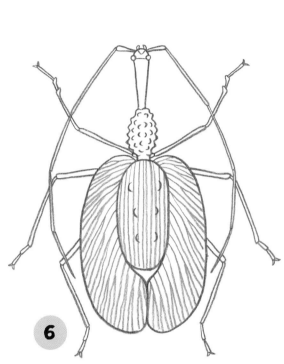

6

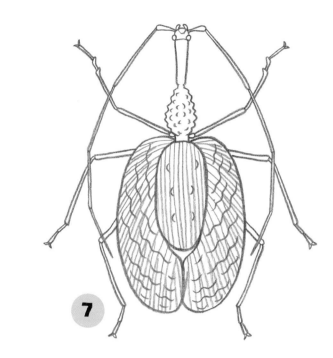

7

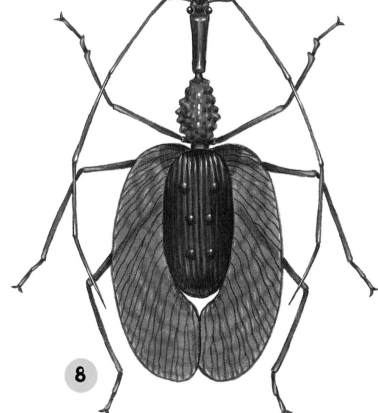

8

fun fact

The violin beetle uses its long bow of a head to search for food in cracks and crevices. It also can squeeze its flat body into tight spaces, allowing it to move freely under soil or even beneath tougher surfaces, such as tree bark.

Cicada

The magicicada species features red eyes and orange wing veins. Its tapered abdomen shape amplifies its music!

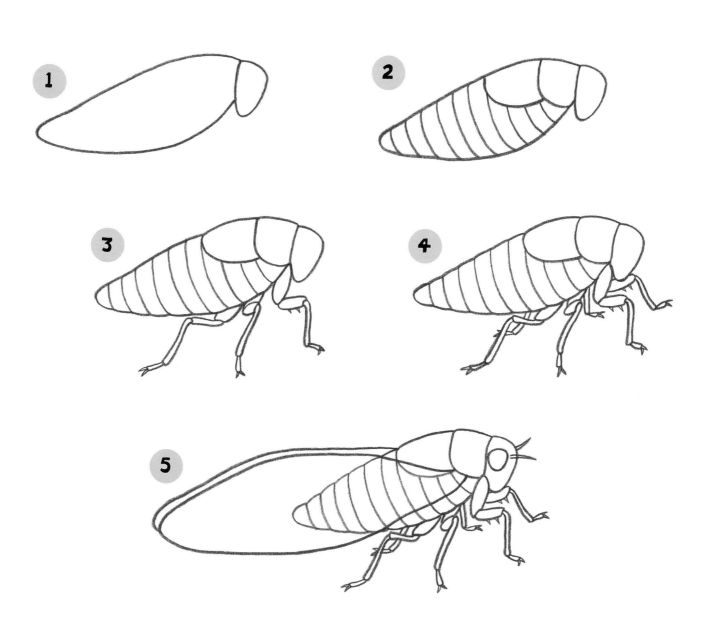

fun fact Groups of magicicada adults emerge in the United States at 13- and 17-year intervals, depending on the brood. After hatching, the young cicadas drop from the trees and crawl underground, where they spend years developing!

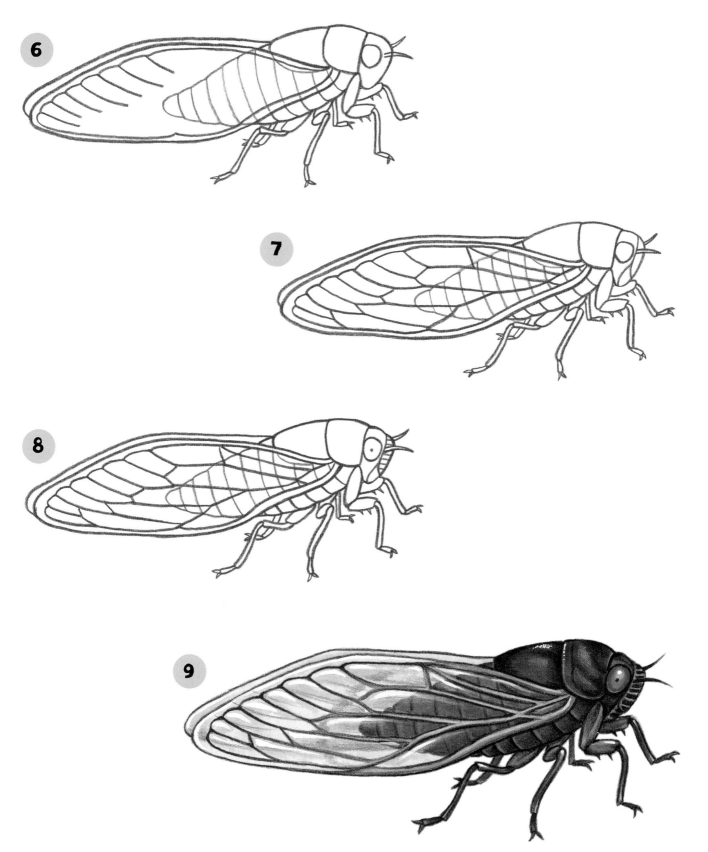

Yellow Jacket Wasp

All social wasps have tiny waists and warning coloration, such as the bright yellow patches that cover this species' black body.

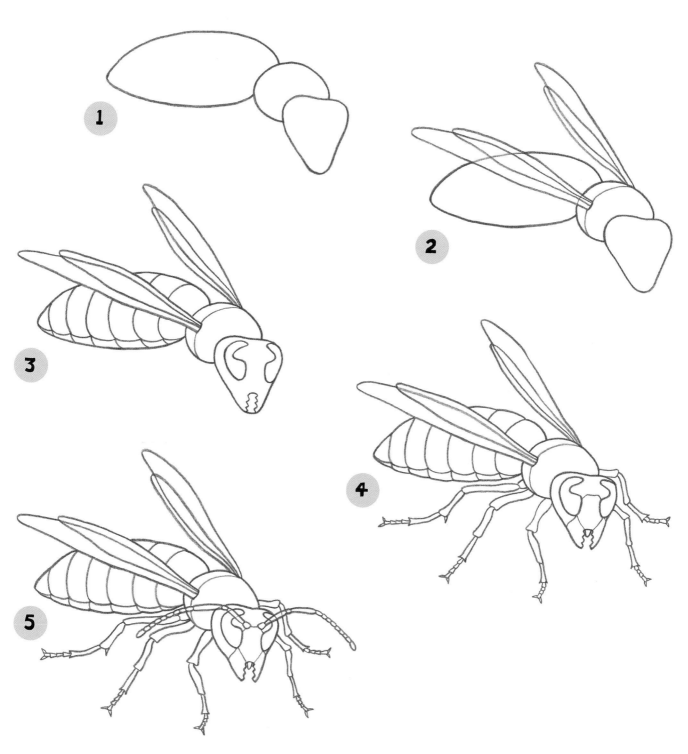

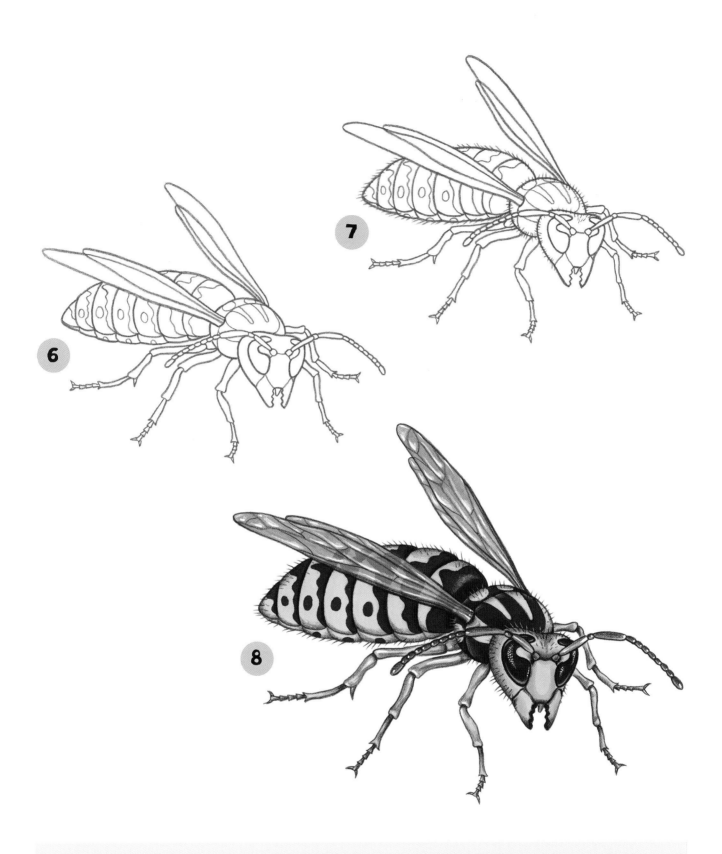

fun fact

The comblike cells of a wasp nest are used to house the wasp eggs and larvae. But because the cells face down and open at the bottom, the queen must glue her eggs inside the cells to keep them from falling out!

Solpugid

A type of sun spider, this desert-dweller
has a hairy body, big chelicerae that act as pincers,
and pedipalps with suction pads!

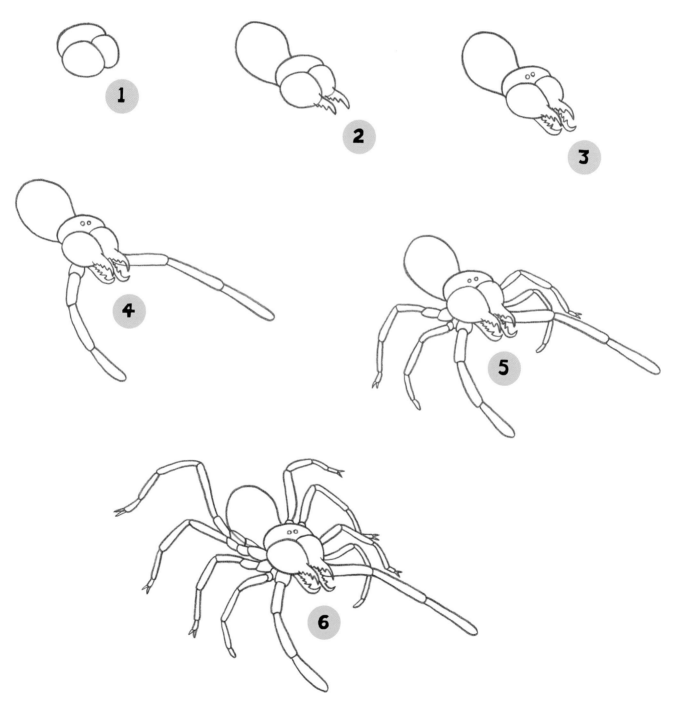

fun fact

The sun spider is also called a "wind scorpion." But despite its names and resemblances, this animal is not related to spiders, scorpions, or other arachnids. It's part of its own order, solifugae, which includes 1,000 species.

Lace Bug

A distinct, lacy wing pattern gives this small gray bug its name. A lacelike plate even extends to hood its head!

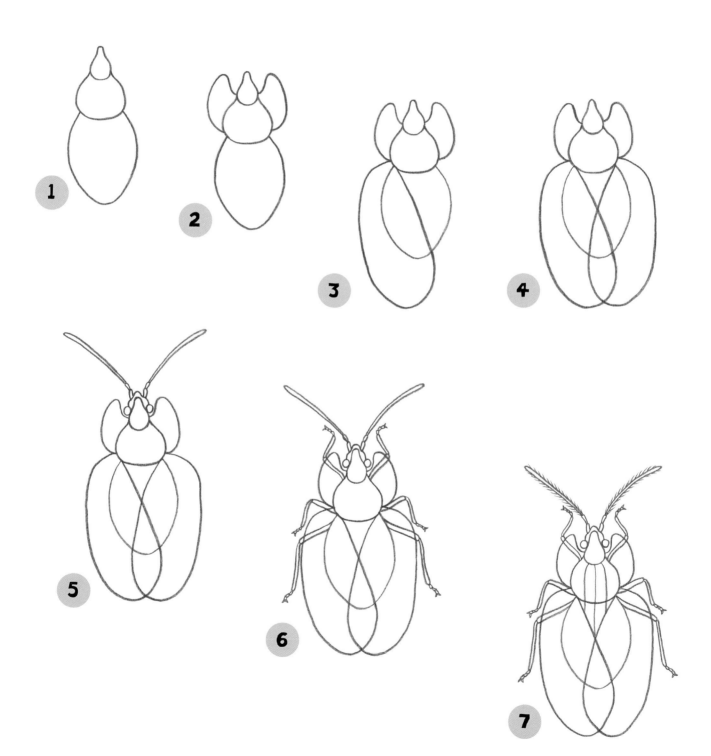

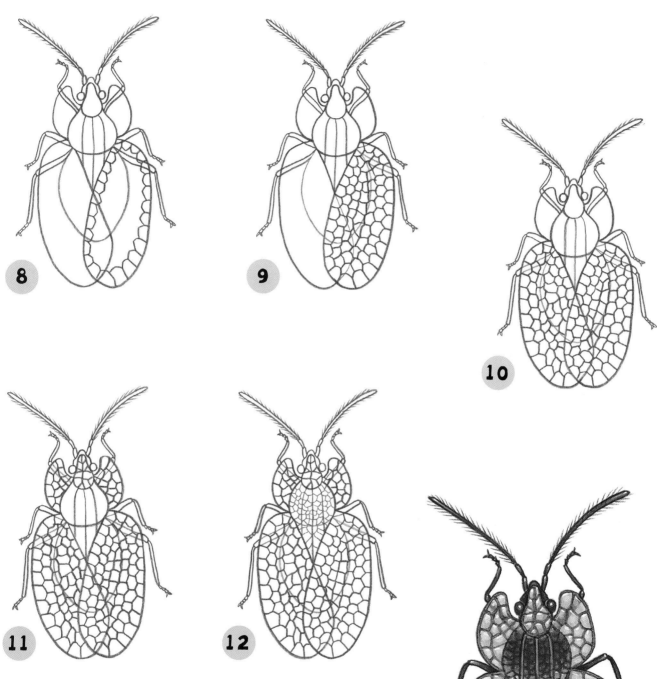

8 9 10 11 12

fun fact

The lace bug may be winged—but that doesn't mean it's a good flier. Its delicate wings are too weak to support its weight long. When it flutters about, it often does so very awkwardly.

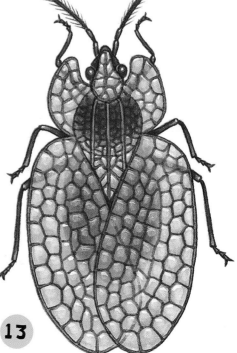

13

Western Honey Bee

One of the smaller bees, this slender, slightly hairy insect is the best known of the honey bees—and it is now found worldwide.

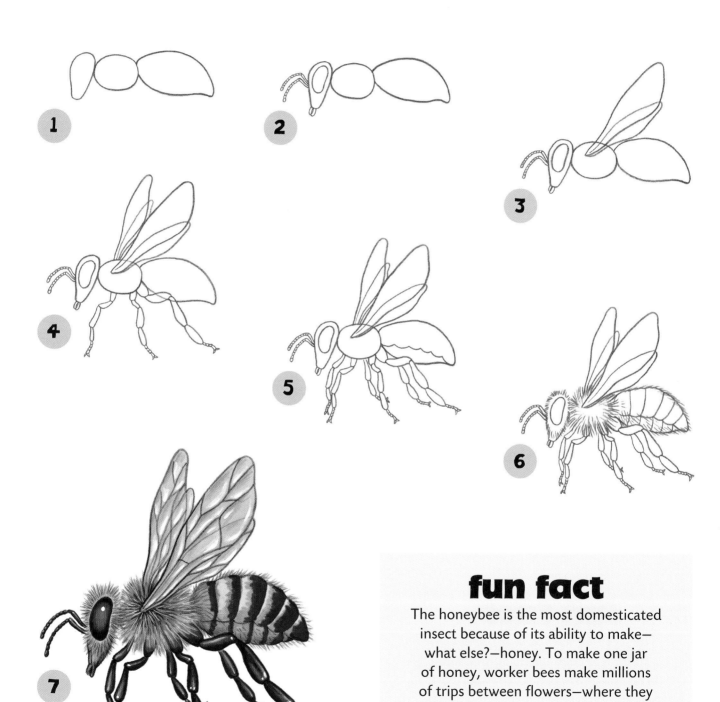

fun fact

The honeybee is the most domesticated insect because of its ability to make— what else?—honey. To make one jar of honey, worker bees make millions of trips between flowers—where they collect nectar—and the hive, where they store their food.